Mark
Twain

ABDO
Publishing Company

by
Sarah Tieck

VISIT US AT
www.abdopublishing.com

Published by ABDO Publishing Company, 8000 West 78th Street, Edina, Minnesota 55439.

Printed in the United States of America, North Mankato, Minnesota
092009
042011

♻ PRINTED ON RECYCLED PAPER

Coordinating Series Editor: Rochelle Baltzer
Contributing Editors: Heidi M.D. Elston, Megan M. Gunderson, BreAnn Rumsch, Marcia Zappa
Graphic Design: Jane Halbert
Cover Photograph: *Getty Images*: Ernest H. Mills
Interior Photographs/Illustrations: *AP Photo*: AP Photo (pp. 5, 25), James A. Finley (pp. 21, 29); *Getty Images*: Jay Colton/Time Life Pictures (p. 15), Hulton Archive (p. 23), Dmitri Kessel/Time Life Pictures (p. 7), Rischgitz (p. 10), Time Life Pictures/Mansell/Time Life Pictures (p. 16) Bert Underwood/George Eastman House (p. 27); *iStockphoto.com*: ©iStockphoto.com/choicegraphx (p. 12), ©iStockphoto.com/JJRD (p. 9); *Mark Twain House and Museum* (pp. 18, 19, 29); *Photos.com* (p. 15).

Library of Congress Cataloging-in-Publication Data

Tieck, Sarah, 1976-
  Mark Twain / Sarah Tieck.
     p. cm. -- (First biographies)
  ISBN 978-1-60453-988-2
  1. Twain, Mark, 1835-1910--Juvenile literature. 2. Authors, American--19th century--Biography--Juvenile literature. I. Title.
  PS1331.T54 2010
  818'.409--dc22
  [B]
                         2009031315

Table of Contents

Who Is Mark Twain? 4

Mark's Family 6

Growing Up 8

Leaving Home 10

Popular Writer 14

Starting a Family 18

Famous Books 20

A Writer's Life 24

Later Years 26

Noted Writer 28

Important Dates 30

Important Words 31

Web Sites 31

Index.. 32

Who Is Mark Twain?

Mark Twain is a famous author. He is known for writing books. Mark lived in a time of many changes. He wrote about what he saw in the world. His writing style changed the way stories are written and read.

One of Mark's most well-known books is *Adventures of Huckleberry Finn*. Another is *The Adventures of Tom Sawyer*.

People still read Mark's books today.

Mark's Family

Mark Twain is the writing name of Samuel Langhorne "Sam" Clemens. Sam was born on November 30, 1835, in Florida, Missouri. His parents were Jane and John Clemens. Sam was the sixth of their seven children.

In 1839, the Clemens family moved to Hannibal, Missouri. John worked as a judge in this growing shipping town. Sam learned about boats. Years later, he would write about what he had seen there.

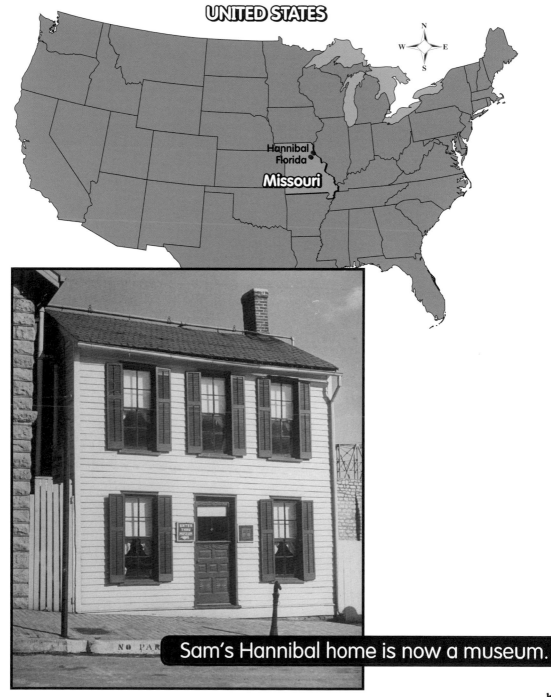

UNITED STATES

Hannibal
Florida
Missouri

Sam's Hannibal home is now a museum.

Growing Up

Sam's life changed when his father died in 1847. To help take care of his family, he started working.

In 1848, Sam became a printer's **apprentice** at a local newspaper. This work helped him discover his love of reading and writing.

One of Sam's jobs at the newspaper was typesetting. He set blocks of letters to print the paper's stories.

Leaving Home

Some of Sam's early work was widely published. But, he wasn't well known right away. He gained fame over time.

By 1851, Sam was writing newspaper articles and making drawings. He was good at writing and drawing, and he enjoyed it. Soon, Sam's work was **published** in newspapers nationwide.

In 1853, Sam began traveling. His travels took him from Missouri to the East Coast. He worked in printing in St. Louis, Missouri, New York City, New York, and Philadelphia, Pennsylvania. And, he continued to write articles and stories.

The name Mark Twain came from Sam's days on the river. This phrase describes water that is 12 feet (3.7 m) deep.

In 1857, Sam began working on riverboats. He was the **apprentice** of a captain. In 1859, Sam became a riverboat **pilot**.

As a pilot, Sam traveled the Mississippi River. His adventures gave him many ideas for writing. His book *Life on the Mississippi* is based on his riverboat days. It was **published** many years later, in 1883.

Popular Writer

In 1861, the **American Civil War** began. The Mississippi River closed to the boats Sam **piloted**.

Sam decided not to fight in the war. So, he traveled to the West with his older brother Orion. Sam had adventures and worked as a reporter. He also wrote short stories.

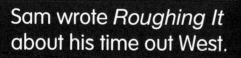

Like many men of his time, Sam searched for silver in the West.

Sam wrote *Roughing It* about his time out West.

The Innocents Abroad is about Sam's adventures in Europe and the Holy Land.

In 1863, Sam began using a different name for his writing. He called himself Mark Twain. He became known for writing funny, exciting stories with strong characters.

Sam traveled to Europe and the **Holy Land** in 1867. Two years later, *The Innocents Abroad* was **published**. Nearly 70,000 copies were sold the first year! It was considered a best seller.

Starting a Family

Mark fell in love with a woman named Olivia Langdon. The couple married on February 2, 1870, in New York. Their son, Langdon, was born later that year. In 1871, the family moved to Hartford, Connecticut.

UNITED STATES

Hartford Connecticut

Mark and Olivia's Hartford home is now a museum. Mark wrote many of his most famous books there.

Langdon died in 1872. But, Mark and Olivia would have three daughters. In 1872, Susy was born. Clara was born in 1874, followed by Jean in 1880.

Mark and Olivia shared many happy times with their daughters.

Famous Books

Mark had many memories of Hannibal and the Mississippi River. He also remembered what life was like before the **American Civil War**. He used these ideas to write two very famous books.

In 1876, *The Adventures of Tom Sawyer* was **published**. It is about a clever and **mischievous** boy named Tom Sawyer. Both children and adults loved Tom and his friend Huck Finn.

There is a statue of Tom and Huck in Hannibal.

In summer 1876, Mark began writing a new story about Huck. In 1885, it was **published** as *Adventures of Huckleberry Finn*. This famous story follows Huck's journey as a runaway.

Many people say *Adventures of Huckleberry Finn* is Mark's most important book.

A Writer's Life

During his life, Mark **published** about 15 major books. He also wrote hundreds of letters and articles. Mark gave many speeches, too.

Soon, Mark and his family became famous. In 1891, they moved to Europe. They traveled all over the world for Mark's work and for fun.

Clara (*left*) and Olivia (*center*) often traveled with Mark.

Later Years

Later in life, Mark faced much sadness. In 1896, Susy died. Then in 1904, Olivia died. Still, Mark continued to travel and write. And, he spent time with Jean and Clara.

In 1908, Mark moved to Redding, Connecticut. Jean died the next year. Mark died soon after, on April 21, 1910. His grave is in New York.

Mark wrote throughout his life.

Noted Writer

Mark wrote so much that new books were **published** after his death! Today, people still read and study his books. Mark Twain is remembered as one of America's finest writers.

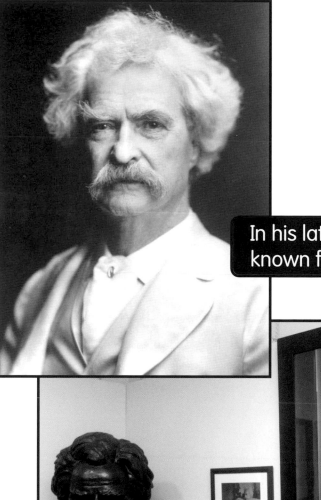

In his later years, Mark became known for wearing a white suit.

Some of Mark's homes are now museums. There, visitors learn about Mark's life.

Important Dates

1835 Mark Twain is born on November 30. His real name is Samuel "Sam" Clemens.

1851 Sam begins writing newspaper articles.

1859 Sam becomes a riverboat pilot.

1861 The American Civil War begins. Sam travels to the West with his older brother Orion.

1863 Sam Clemens begins writing as Mark Twain.

1869 *The Innocents Abroad* is published.

1870 Mark marries Olivia Langdon. Over the years, Mark and Olivia would have four children.

1876 *The Adventures of Tom Sawyer* is published.

1883 *Life on the Mississippi* is published.

1885 *Adventures of Huckleberry Finn* is published.

1910 Mark Twain dies on April 21.

Important Words

American Civil War the war between the Northern and Southern states from 1861 to 1865.

apprentice (uh-PREHN-tuhs) a person who learns a trade or a craft from a skilled worker.

Holy Land an area in the Middle East considered important to many religions. It is currently in Palestine.

mischievous (MIHS-chuh-vuhs) playfully causing trouble.

pilot someone whose job is to direct a ship. To pilot is to direct a ship.

publish to print the work of an author.

Web Sites

To learn more about Mark Twain, visit ABDO Publishing Company online. Web sites about Mark Twain are featured on our Book Links page. These links are routinely monitored and updated to provide the most current information available.

www.abdopublishing.com

Index

Adventures of Huckleberry Finn **4, 22, 23, 30**

Adventures of Tom Sawyer, The **4, 20, 30**

American Civil War **14, 20, 30**

Clemens, Clara **19, 24, 25, 26, 30**

Clemens, Jane **6**

Clemens, Jean **19, 24, 26, 30**

Clemens, John **6, 8**

Clemens, Langdon **18, 19, 30**

Clemens, Olivia (Langdon) **18, 19, 24, 25, 26, 30**

Clemens, Orion **14, 30**

Clemens, Susy **19, 24, 26, 30**

Connecticut **18, 26**

Europe **16, 17, 24**

Holy Land **16, 17**

Innocents Abroad, The **16, 17, 30**

Life on the Mississippi **13, 30**

Mississippi River **12, 13, 14, 20**

Missouri **6, 7, 11, 20, 21**

New York **11, 18, 26**

Pennsylvania **11**

Roughing It **15**